Spirit of
Summit County

Colorado

Though we travel the world over
to find the beautiful,
we must carry it with us
or we find it not.
R.W. Emerson

SPIRIT OF SUMMIT COUNTY

COLORADO

A PHOTOGRAPHIC CELEBRATION

For Claire —
Thanks for helping
with the Queens College
alumni campaign!
Christine Beck '64

Christine Safford Beck

PrismLight PRESS

Library of Congress Card Number: 95-71871
ISBN 0-9649005-0-5

Published by PrismLight Press
P.O. Box 766, Bryn Mawr, PA 19010, phone: 610-525-1973

Art Direction and Graphic Design by Cristina Lazar

Sincere thanks to the following for granting permission to reproduce quotations: Ansel Adams, Reprinted by permission of The Ansel Adams Publishing Rights Trust from *Ansel Adams, Our National Parks,* Copyright 1992. Margaret Holley, "Little Mind, Big Mind" from *Beyond Me, Voices of the Natural World,* North Word Press Inc. Copyright 1993 by Christine Safford Beck and Margaret Holley. Reprinted by permission. Excerpt from *John of the Mountains,* edited by Linnie Marsh Wolfe. Copyright 1938 by Wanda Muir Hanna. Copyright © renewed 1966 by John Muir Hanna and Ralph Eugene Wolfe. Reprinted by permission of Houghton Mifflin Company. All rights reserved.

ACKNOWLEDGEMENTS
Special thanks to:
Greg della Stua and Lori Comtois of PrintNet for book production, for their patient explanations and for making it possible to go full-speed ahead;
Cristina Lazar for her sensitive creativity, tireless commitment and advice;
Jeanne Moutoussamy-Ashe for her kind words and friendship;
Karel Hayes for drawing the map;
The many people in Summit County who offered help and encouragement, especially Sue Miller of the U.S.Forest Service, Dori Webb at Summit County Offices, Deb Edwards of The Summit Foundation, Currie Craven, and everyone at the Summit County Chamber of Commerce;
All my friends, especially Maggie Holley, Charlene Guyer and Betsy Sussman who are always willing to offer encouragement and ideas;
And to my family: my mother for her understanding; Lars for his title ideas; Eric and Anders for their interest and patience; and most of all to Leif for his encouragement, editing and standards of excellence.

Creative technical advice: Lorel Danzig
Layout assistance: Marisol Quintana Galetovic
Many thanks to: Maria Toth, Margaret & Mark Garrison, Patita P. Scott, Barbara Seidel, Adrian Hass, Lynn Harvy, Ioan Horea, Ran & Kira della Stua.
Printing through PrintNet in Hong Kong.

CONTENTS

PREFACE

We come to the mountains for many different reasons. When we must leave, we take away new memories, new mental images and new feelings that will stay with us. And we know we'll be back.

Whether we come to take adventurous risks or simply to relax, whether we come to ski, to fish, to hike, to picnic by alpine lakes or to ascend four-teeners, our senses are touched. In spite of our diversity, there is common ground - a universality - in what these mountains inspire in us. At some level and at certain moments, you feel what I feel and vice versa.

As a photographer, I am necessarily involved with what is visible, what is seen. Thus, a well-exe-cuted, well-composed portrait of a beautiful or dra-matic subject makes a strong impact. However, my real challenge is capturing on film something of the invisible, the unseen. The intangibles, the things of the heart and mind and spirit are, for each of us, most significant and most enduring. That is why I photograph.

That is also what makes these mountains so spe-cial. We cannot help but feel awe and wonder - as we experience the quiet beauty of the Arapaho National Forest, as we feel icy snow on our faces, as we take in the drama of majestic vistas, as we see the power of blizzards and thunder and lightning, as we sense the energy of the people here and their "connected-ness" to the outdoors. These experi-ences, personal yet universal, make up the very spir-it of Summit County.

I love this County's diversity - its vibrant ener-gy, its history, the risks and challenges inherent in the terrain and high altitude, as well as the peace of special, quiet places. I feel refreshed and energized here, exhilarated and at peace, all at the same time. I know you feel all of this, too, because these mountains are full of energy, color. . . and spirit.

While we savor the present, we must also think about the future. The rapid growth of Summit County's ski slopes, towns, resorts and traffic cre-ates new issues of safety and control; so in the same way we must hear the call of the snow-covered forests and of the alpine flowers to care for them, to keep them safe too.

With this book I hope to help preserve the spirit of Summit County and share a bit of my vision of this region's magic. It is a jewel in the Colorado Rockies.

C.S.B.

SPIRIT OF THE SUMMIT
ADVENTURE, FREEDOM AND REFLECTION

The lure of precious metals and a spirit of adventure brought streams of settlers in the mid 19th century and planted the seed of Summit County. Although Ute Indians hunted buffalo here and fur trappers and traders knew the area, the discovery of gold in 1859 started a wave.

Small mining towns and camps popped up, and the spirit of Summit County began. New freedoms were experienced. New ground was forged. Fortunes were made, and hardships endured. Railroads were built. The mountains were thought to be conquered.

However, after the boom came the bust with the collapse of the silver market in 1893. Many bustling towns turned into ghost towns. The mountains became quiet again.

Halfway into the 20th century, the same spirit of adventure and lure that founded the earliest mining communities surfaced again, this time because of the magical "white gold" - *SNOW*.

The Summit's first ski area, Arapahoe Basin, opened in 1946, and the power of white gold took hold as three more major mountains welcomed skiers. Currently, Summit County boasts four inter-nationally acclaimed ski resorts, each with its own flavor, A-Basin, Breckenridge, Copper Mountain and Keystone. With each so accessible to the others, millions of winter visitors come to "Ski the Summit."

And the spirit grows. The magic of gold takes on rainbow qualities as more and more people discover the glories of summer and fall in Summit County. Arapaho National Forest's dramatic terrain encour-ages diverse outdoor activities ranging from physi-cally exhausting challenges to peaceful alpine soli-tude. No wonder the County attracts a growing number of residents, visitors, conferences and con-certs and special events.

This spirit of Summit County - of adventure, of freedom, of reflection - reaches out, inspiring, moti-vating and challenging us.

"Teach your children what we have taught our children - that the earth is our mother. Whatever befalls the earth befalls the sons and daughters of the earth. If men spit upon the ground, they spit upon themselves.

This we know. The earth does not belong to us; we belong to the earth. This we know. All things are connected like the blood which unites one family. All things are connected..."

Chief Seattle

---

7. Girl with a kite at Kingdom Park.
8. Bumper sticker on car at Copper Mountain.

9. Litter sign at Meadow Creek Trailhead.

10. A baby spruce lifts its branches out of the snow.

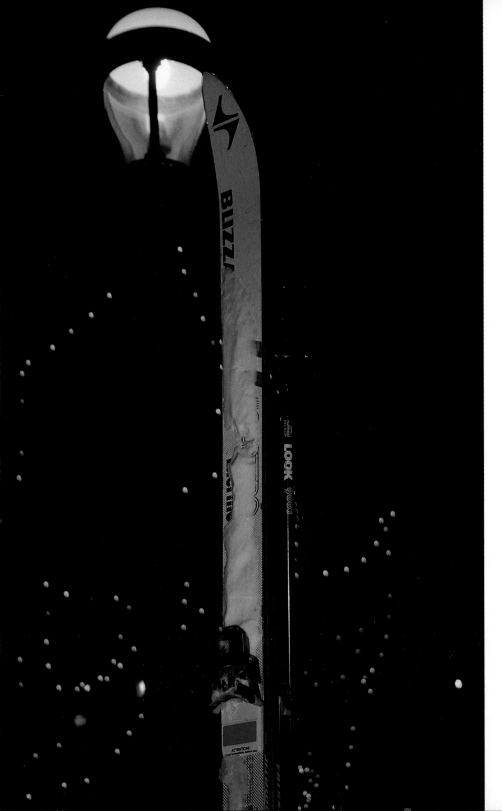

"Each bootprint behind me is someone's

I used to be,

and my mind is as still as the mountains,

and I am their speech."

Margaret Holley

11. Skis by lamppost.
12. Shoveled path in Dillon.

13. A blizzard mutes the vivid colors of ski clothes in the lift line.

14. Skiers at Arapahoe Basin Ski Area, Summit County's first and highest.

The clear, clean mountain air energizes joggers and exercise enthusiasts. Most visitors, however, need time to acclimate to the high altitude. Summit County's towns range from 9,000' above sea level in Silverthorne to 10,268' in Montezuma.

15. Jogger

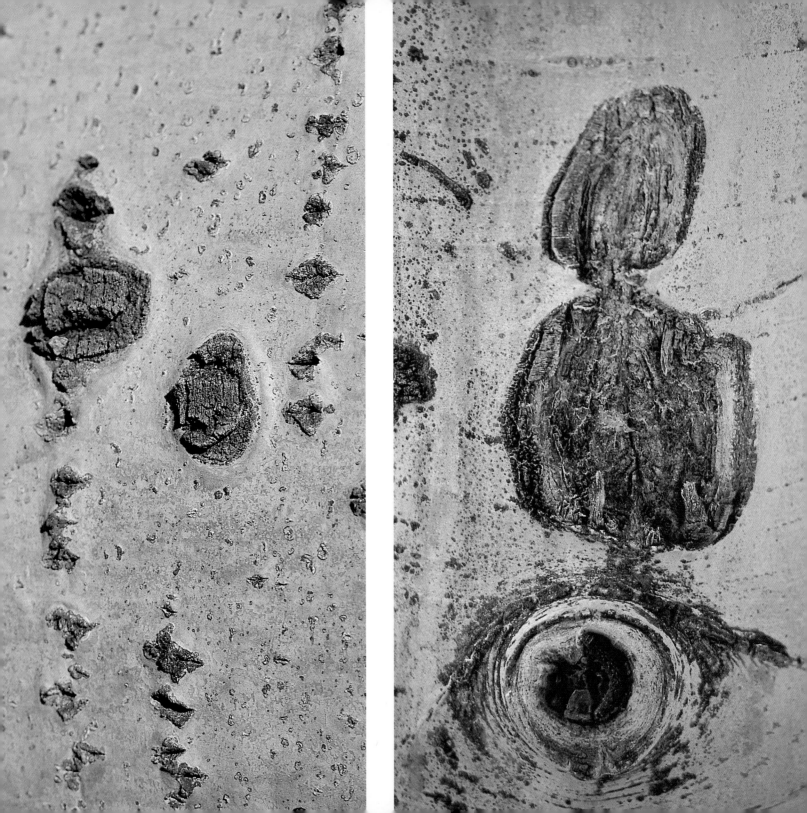

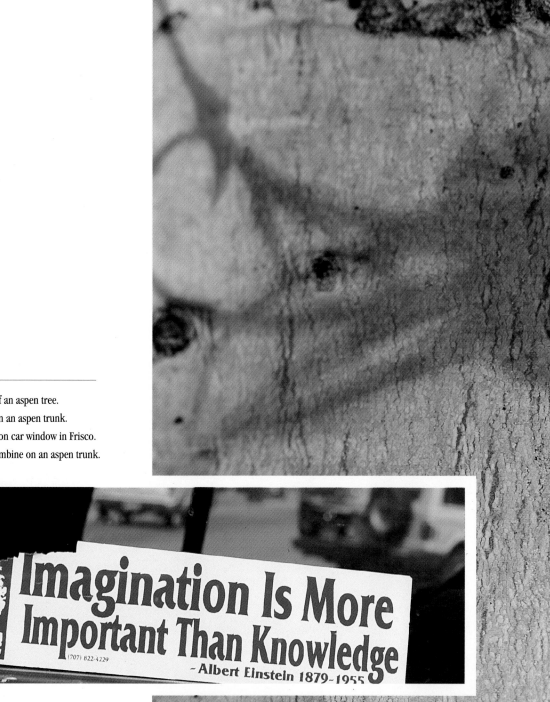

16. Bark of an aspen tree.

17. Mystery on an aspen trunk.

18. Bumper sticker on car window in Frisco.

19. Shadow of a Columbine on an aspen trunk.

20. Reflections in base lodge window,
Arapahoe Basin.

21. Reflections in a store window,
Breckenridge.

THE SUMMIT'S MANY COLORS

ON THE MOUNTAINS AND IN THE TOWNS

In the winter, bright colors on the ski mountain enliven the season's whites and greens.

Summer surprises of every color of the rainbow brighten the dominant greens, browns and blues.

Nature combines yellows, pinks, lavenders, oranges and blues in ways not bound by human creativity.

25. Young skier in red.

26. Skier on the moguls.

27. Brightly colored flags at A-Basin.

Arapahoe Basin has earned its nickname "The Legend." With a summit elevation of 13,050' it usually stays open until June. In 1995 it set a record keeping two runs open into August.

28. The pin on the 6th hole, Copper Creek Golf Course.

29. Yellow pond lily, Lily Pad Lake.

30. Grasses in pond.

With an eye made quiet by the power
Of harmony, and the deep power of joy,
We see into the life of things.

William Wordsworth

31. Yellow boat and grasses, Dillon Marina.

32. Field of Oxeye Daisies near Cataract Lake.

33. Baskets of summer flowers grace Breckenridge's light post.

Although the Blue Columbine looks delicate and fragile, it thrives naturally in the harsh conditions and short growing season of high-altitude terrain. Beautiful Columbine bouquets appear in alpine meadows, on rocky hillsides, at the edge of evergreen forests and in aspen groves. These Columbine, in all their splendor, were in the Eagles Nest Wilderness area near the Boss Mine.

34. Columbine banners, Copper Mountain Resort.
35. Columbine bouquets on Rock Creek Trail.
36 Blue Columbine, Colorado's state flower.

37. Fireweed, Arapaho National Forest.
38. Lupine in meadow, Arapaho
National Forest.
39. Fireweed colors around the poppies.

▲

40. Thistles by the Green Mountain Reservoir near the town of Heeney.

41. Reflections in pond, Keystone Resort.

45. Sunset at Lake Dillon.

46. Lupine by the dirt road to Meadow Creek Trailhead.

47. Lupine.

48. Stemless Golden Weed and lichen,
    Arapaho National Forest.

49. Continental Falls on the Mohawk
    Lakes Trail.

50. Indian Paintbrush through forest green.

51. Stop sign on Main Street, Montezuma.

52. Every fall, the hills are ablaze with the golden glow of the aspen trees.

53. Illusion in an aspen grove.

54. Alpine sunflowers in Black Powder Pass with view of Tenmile Range, page56/57.

WHITE GOLD...SNOW AT THE SUMMIT

ENERGETIC SKIING AND QUIET FORESTS

"In the mountains we forget to count the days," says a Japanese proverb. That may hold true generally, but not as ski season approaches.

Enthusiastic skiers welcome the first snowfall and dream of fresh powder. Others count the days until they can experience once again the remarkable quiet, deep in a snow-covered forest.

Praises are sung for the 10 ski mountains, the 60 lifts that can wisk 84,268 skiers per hour to the 374 runs at the County's four ski areas:

▲ ARAPAHOE BASIN with its legendary challenges above timberline;

▲ BRECKENRIDGE with its four contiguous, magnificent mountains;

▲ COPPER MOUNTAIN with its gorgeous, naturally separated terrain; and

▲ KEYSTONE with its three diverse mountains and unique night skiing.

Nordic centers in Frisco, as well as Breckenridge, Copper Mountain and Keystone, open the doors to hundreds of miles of cross country trails. Winter at the Summit also provides ice-skating, sleigh rides, snowmobiling and fun-in-the-snow limited only by your imagination.

And the stillness, the quiet, deep in a snow-covered forest, defies description.

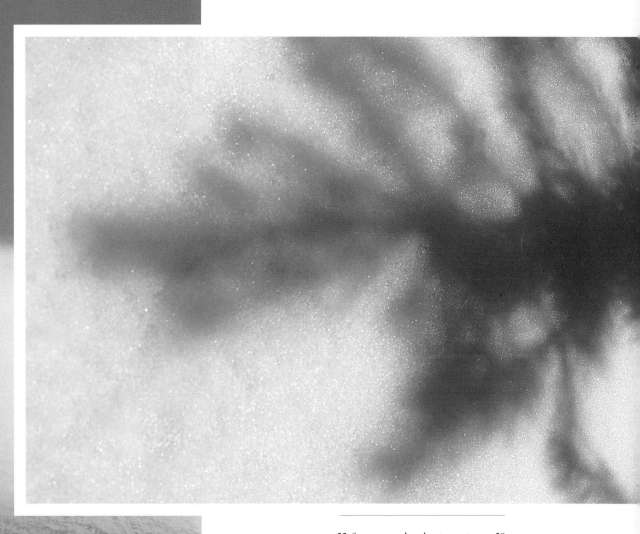

55. Snow-covered peaks at sunset, page 58

56. Couds hanging over peaks, viewed from Monte Cristo Gulch

57. Shadow of tree branch on snow.

With Quandary Peak soaring above the Blue Lakes valley, the winter solitude contrasts the action on the ski slopes.

58. Winter hiker by Quandary Peak.
59. Tracks in the snow and cross-country skier on Lake Dillon.

61. Fallen aspen leaf in the snow.

62. Grasses appearing through the snow.

63. Aspen grove in winter, Eagles Nest Wilderness.

60. Snow covered Monte Cristo Gulch by Quandary, page 64/65.

64. Snow covered Quandary Peak.

65. Grays and Torreys Peaks.

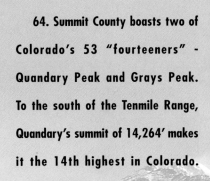

64. Summit County boasts two of Colorado's 53 "fourteeners" - Quandary Peak and Grays Peak. To the south of the Tenmile Range, Quandary's summit of 14,264' makes it the 14th highest in Colorado.

65. Both fourteeners, Grays and Torreys Peaks look like twins but only Grays is in Summit County. Grays Peak is the state's ninth highest with a summit of 14,270', three feet higher than Torreys.

66. Silverthorne and distinctive Buffalo Mountain.

67. Ice skating on the pond, Keystone Resort.

68. Sunbeams on a Breckenridge chair lift.

69. Skier on mountain at Keystone.

70. From one of Summit County's
60 chair lifts.

71. Snowboarder taking a break.

71a. Rack full of skis at mid-mountain.

72. Atop Peak 9, Breckenridge Ski Area.

73. The popular Popcorn Wagon at Copper Mountain Ski Area.

74. Ice-covered evergreen needles.
75. Frisco's Historic Park preserves the old schoolhouse, jail and log cabins.

76. Silverthorne, often called the "hometown" of Summit County, boasts a huge variety of factory outlet stores.

77. Snowy forest.

78. Snow-covered rooftop against the Tenmile Range, Dillon.

79. Peak 1, a familiar site from Route 9 , towers over Summit County.

80. Bald Mountain, 13,684' and affectionately known as "Baldy," soars over Breckenridge.

GREENS AND BLUES ARE GOLDEN, TOO

SUMMER'S COLORS AND ACTIVE PLAY

Nature's beauty fills the soul year-round in the mountains, but summer and fall have their own special splendor. Without snow cover, the high country is full of contrast and contradiction.

Monotone greens and browns, offset by "Colorado blue" sky, dominate the rugged terrain. Depending on the light and time of day, the creeks and waterfalls often appear brownish, though usually sparkling. The color of the alpine lakes and reservoirs changes with the sky.

Amid harsh high-country terrain, the beauty of new delicate growth by a rushing stream seems even more miraculous. The greens are rich, and the tiny flowers welcome us.

Vast peaks, rugged rocks, scree and dirt surround wildflowers in nature's unmatched colors. The vista and the details draw smiles and wonder. In autumn, the brilliance of the aspen trees leaves no question about the richness of real gold.

Recreational activities - and food for the body and soul - abound as summer-colored "gold" works its magic.

Indians, explorers and settlers surely experienced the peace of aspen groves. Now, tourists, hikers and cross country skiers appreciate it too. The Quaking Aspen tree, Colorado's member of the poplar family, has delicate leaves that flutter in the faintest wind and turn a glorious golden color every autumn.

81. Mariposa Lily, page 84.
82. Shadows of daisies on aspen trunk.
87. Aspen grove with Queen Anne's Lace, Arapaho National Forest.

▲
87

84. Lake Dillon through a rain-soaked window at Giberson Bay.

85. Storm clouds over Clinton Peak, south of Copper Mountain.

86. Reflections at Officers Gulch.

87. Ducks at Keystone Resort.

▲

Peace at Lower Cataract Lake in Eagles Nest Wilderness, off a dirt road from Heeney Road, 16 miles north of Silverthorne. Hundreds of lakes like this one provide a solitary place to relax and reflect. Several challenging hiking trails start here and lead to secluded alpine lakes.

John Muir wrote, " These beautiful days must enrich all my life. They do not exist as mere pictures - maps hung upon the walls of memory....They saturate themselves into every part of the body and live always."

89. Frisco.

90. Heeney and Green Mountain Reservoir.

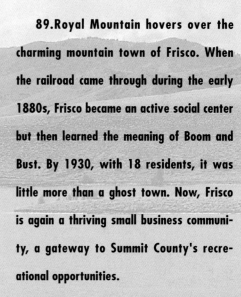

89. Royal Mountain hovers over the charming mountain town of Frisco. When the railroad came through during the early 1880s, Frisco became an active social center but then learned the meaning of Boom and Bust. By 1930, with 18 residents, it was little more than a ghost town. Now, Frisco is again a thriving small business community, a gateway to Summit County's recreational opportunities.

90. The small town of Heeney, in the County's northern corner, sits idylically on the edge of the Green Mountain Reservoir. Heeney is well-known for its annual Tick Festival.

▲

91. Sailboats on Lake Dillon from the Sapphire
Point loop trail, page 96.

92. Sailboats at Frisco's marina, page 97.

93. A grand vista of Keller Mountain from Boss
Mine in Eagles Nest Wilderness.

94. Backpacks by the pilings of old Boss Mine.

95. Indian Paintbrush Bud.

▲

96. Bikers.

Over 50 miles of paved bike trails connect Copper Mountain with Frisco, Silverthorne, Dillon and Breckenridge. The trail winds along the Tenmile Creek, the edge of Lake Dillon, and south along the Blue River. Bikers can also continue west out of Summit County over Vail Pass.

Summit County also boasts over 400 miles of dirt roads and trails open to mountain biking.

97. Tenmile Range hovering over Wheeler Junction, a familiar vista along I-70.

98. Clouds.

99. Father Dyer on a church window in Breckenridge.

An itinerant preacher in the late 1880s, he traveled across the passes on snowshoes.

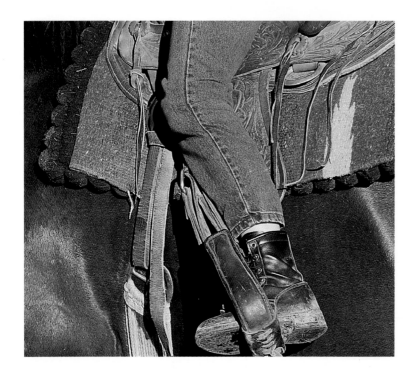

100.Old carriage at Keystone's stables.

101. On horseback.

101a. Horseback riders at Keystone.

102. Horseback riders at Eagles Nest Wilderness.

103. Boreas Pass Road, open to motor vehicles in the summer, leads to the Continental Divide and on to Como. In the late 1800s the Denver, South Park and Pacific Railroad's line across Boreas Pass made Breckenridge a supply and transportation center.

104. A meadow ridge in Black Powder Pass, accessible on foot from the top of Boreas Pass Road.

"You must have certain noble areas of the world left in as close-to-primal condition as possible. You must have quietness and a certain amount of solitude. You must be able to touch the living rock, drink the pure waters, scan the great vistas, sleep under the stars and awaken to the cool dawn wind. Such experiences are the heritage of all people."

Ansel Adams

105. Field of flowers, Arapaho National Forest.

106. Trees and trunks at the Continental Divide.

▲

107. Hikers in Black Powder Pass.

108. Waterfall in McCullough Gulch.

Rich in mining history, waterfalls and spectacular views, McCullough Gulch is a popular hiking area.

▲

113. Curtain Ponds by 1-70 at Wheeler Junction and by Copper Mountain.

114. Cabin by Last Dollar Mine in McCullough Gulch.

115. Creative bird-feeder, Last Dollar Mine.

116. Marmot, Arapaho National Forest.

117. Families ready to raft the river waters.

118. Women hikers by Lily Pad Lake, page 120/121.

119. Pink poppy, page 121.

120. Snow-covered cliff, Arapaho National Forest, page 122.

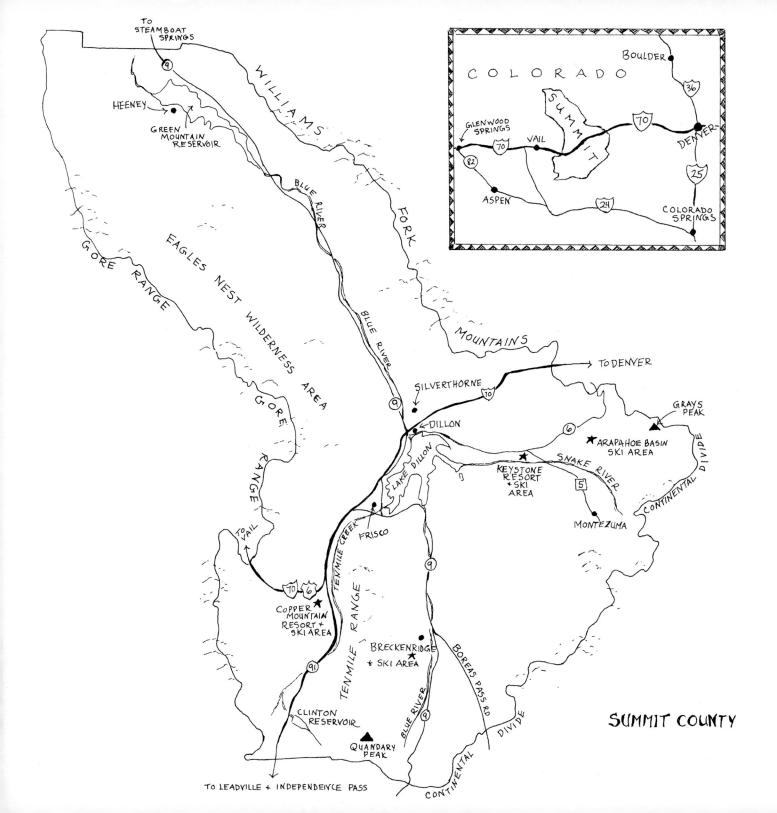

ABOUT THE COUNTY
Capsule Descriptions of its Towns, Ski Areas and Natural Features

ARAPAHO NATIONAL FOREST, sets the backdrop for Summit County's diversity. "Named peaks" in the County total 76, including 25 peaks over 13,000' and two of Colorado's 53 legendary "fourteeners," Grays Peak and Quandary Peak. The National Forest also features campsites, mineshafts and remains of mining camps, ghost towns and hundreds of hiking, mountain biking, horseback riding, four-wheel drive and cross-country ski trails.

ARAPAHOE BASIN SKI AREA, founded in 1946, boasts 490 acres of challenging skiing in bowls above timberline. With a base elevation of 10,800' and a summit elevation of 13,050', A-Basin's average annual snowfall is 360 inches, giving it the longest ski season in the County, usually until mid-June. Its spectacular terrain, including "The East Wall," has earned it the nickname The Legend.

BLUE RIVER, incorporated as a town in the mid 1960's, remains a quiet residential community south of Breckenridge. Along with mountains, forests and streams, Gosse Pasture Tarn is one of its features.

THE BLUE RIVER, offering excellent trout fishing, flows through the towns of Blue River, Breckenridge and Silverthorne. From Silverthorne to the Colorado River, the Blue has been designated a Gold Medal fishing stream. Its rapids also provide river rafting thrills.

BRECKENRIDGE, Colorado's oldest Western Slope community with an altitude of 9,600', obtained its first post office in 1859. Named after then Vice President John C. Breckinridge, the spelling was later changed to acknowledge the Union victory and to express outrage at the Vice President's pro-Confederate stance and his conviction of treason. In 1980 Breckenridge was designated a National Historic District with over 230 examples of mining town architecture. The Summit Historical Society focuses on preserving these original buildings, dating from the 1800s. Today the town features shops, galleries, lodges and resorts, restaurants, a new Recreation Center, the Riverwalk Center for summertime concerts, an acclaimed Jack Nicklaus-designed golf course and numerous special events.

BRECKENRIDGE SKI AREA, first open to skiers in December, 1961, features 1,915 acres of skiable terrain on four contiguous mountains of the Tenmile Range Peaks 7, 8, 9 and 10. With over 70 miles of trails as well as challenging bowls, its longest run is 3 1/2 miles long. Of the four

mountains, Peak 8 has the highest summit elevation at 12,998'. The Breckenridge Nordic Center and ice skating on Maggie Pond also provide popular winter activities.

The CONTINENTAL DIVIDE runs through Colorado's Rocky Mountains. Streams east of the Divide flow into the Atlantic Ocean, and streams west of it flow into the Pacific. The Continental Divide serves as the Summit County boundary from just north of Grays Peak on the east all the way to Hoosier Pass on the south.

COPPER MOUNTAIN RESORT, which opened in 1972, was the fruition of the dreams of Judge John S. Wheeler one hundred years earlier. The judge founded Wheeler Station, where Copper Mountain Resort stands today, as a mining and logging camp but expressed the vision of its becoming a successful resort someday. In addition to the ski mountains, dozens of summer activities are available on West Lake and in the mountainous terrain, including the Pete and Perry Dye-designed highest championship golf course in North America.

COPPER MOUNTAIN SKI AREA, which also opened in 1972 with luxurious Copper Mountain Resort at its base, boasts expansion into Copper Bowl to give 1,860 skiable acres plus upgraded, highspeed lifts. With 98 trails and four bowls, Copper is the only Colorado ski resort with a "naturally divided terrain." Its high summit is atop Copper Peak, at 12,441', though Union Peak is almost as high. Ice skating and cross country skiing are also popular in the winter.

DILLON, nestled at the edge of Lake Dillon and 9,017' above sea level, is a resort town and active cultural arts center with grand vistas of the Tenmile Range. The original town sits under water on the south side of Lake Dillon. When Denver's growing need for water necessitated a new dam site in the early 1960s, Dillon residents relocated by moving entire homes and businesses. The Summit Historical Society Museum, located in the old Dillon School House, helps to preserve the area's history.

EAGLES NEST WILDERNESS AREA, 133,688 acres of high country within Arapaho National Forest, encompasses the Gore Range and within Summit County stretches from Copper Mountain all the way north almost to Heeney. Trails, alpine lakes and spectacular vistas abound.

FRISCO, 9,096' high on the western end of Lake Dillon, is a thriving resort and business community. With Mount Royal hovering above, Frisco serves as a gateway to the County's diverse recreational activities. When the railroads came through in the early 1880s, Frisco, like Dillon, became an active social and trade center. Having survived its near-ghost-town status after the mining heydays, Frisco preserves its frontier past with a Historic Park and Museum maintained by the Frisco Historical Society, In the winter, Frisco's Nordic Center is popular for cross country skiers.

THE GORE RANGE, which forms the western boundary of the County's northern arm, features dramatic high country trails, lakes and waterfalls.

GRAYS PEAK, Colorado's ninth highest peak, soars 14,270' next to its twin peak, Torreys, which is in neighboring Clear Creek County. Named for Asa Gray, a botanist and national authority on flora and fauna, Grays Peak is a popular day trek. Since a ridge connects the summit of Grays Peak with that of Torreys, these peaks give hikers the chance to climb two "fourteeners" in one day. Hikers should start out early to avoid being on the summit when the common afternoon thunderstorms roll in. A good supply of water and a warm jacket are necessities as well.

GREEN MOUNTAIN RESERVOIR, a recreational haven in the northern arm of the County, has Rainbow Trout and Kokanee Salmon in its waters and six campgrounds on its shores. Boating, waterskiing and jet-skiing are also popular. This reservoir was completed in 1943 as part of the Colorado-Big Thompson Project.

HEENEY, a little residential town built into a hillside at the edge of the Green Mountain Reservoir and amid spacious ranch land, has a boat ramp, dock and idyllic views. First settled when the Big Thompson Project began, Heeney was named for landowner Paul Heeney. Every year the town celebrates by hosting the Heeney Tick Festival.

KEYSTONE RESORT, in the Snake River Valley with many reminders of the area's silver mining past, offers dozens of year-round activities. Unlimited summer recreation includes golf on its acclaimed Robert Trent Jones, Jr. course. When completed, The Village of River Run combined with Ski Tip Ranch, site of the Ski Tip stage stop in the 1860s, will provide a new dimension.

KEYSTONE SKI AREA, which first welcomed skiers in 1970, features 1,737 acres on three distinctly different mountains: Keystone, North Peak and Outback. Unique night skiing is possible on over 34% of Keystone Mountain. With 89 trails, two bowls and 100% snowmaking

capability, Keystone's highest summit of 12,200' is on The Outback. Ice skating on Keystone Pond and cross country skiing are also popular.

LAKE DILLON, a man-made reservoir in the center of Summit County, was created in the early 1960s to help meet Denver's growing need for water. Fed by the Snake River, the Blue River and the Tenmile Creek, it features 3,300 acres with 25 miles of shoreline. Its two marinas, in Dillon and Frisco, are among the world's highest.

MONTEZUMA, Summit County's smallest and highest town at 10,268', is a mecca for outdoor enthusiasts. Nearby Saints John is a relic of a silver mining community.

QUANDARY PEAK, at the southern end of the Tenmile Range, is Colorado's 14th highest summit at 14,264'. A heavily mined mountain, it was apparently named because early miners were "in a quandary" trying to identify some unusual rocks discovered near the summit. Today Quandary is a popular day-trek that takes about four hours to ascend. Hikers should start out early with the goal of being off the summit and headed toward treeline before afternoon thunderstorms roll in. A good supply of water and warm clothes are necessities also.

SILVERTHORNE, the County's largest and lowest town at 9,000', features a thriving year-round community and the Silverthorne Factory Outlet Stores. As the gateway to Arapaho National Forest and home to the U.S. Forest Service Information Center, Silverthorne boasts spectacular views of the Williams Fork Mountains, the Gore Range and distinctive Buffalo Mountain, as well as the Tenmile Range. Construction of Lake Dillon and the Eisenhower Tunnel in the 1960s essentially created the town, named for the widely respected Judge Marshall Silverthorne. A spectacular golf course and a new state-of-the-art recreation center add more opportunities.

The SNAKE RIVER flows through Montezuma and Keystone into Lake Dillon.

The TENMILE RANGE stretches from Frisco down past Breckenridge almost to the southern edge of the County. This range is home to many hiking and cross-country trails, old mines, Breckenridge's ski area on Peaks 7, 8, 9 and 10, and Quandary Peak, one of the County's two fourteeners.

WILLIAMS FORK MOUNTAINS form the eastern boundary of the County's northern arm.

THE ENVIRONMENT
Groups that Care

Many volunteers and organizations are actively involved in preserving Summit County for the future. Some of them are listed here if you want to get involved.

Breckenridge Fat Tire Society,
    Box 2845, Breckenridge
Breckenridge Outdoor Education Center,
    (970) 453-6422
Breckenridge Ski Touring Society
Colorado Avalanche Information Center
    (303) 371-1080
Colorado Bird Observatory (303) 659-4348
Colorado Division of Wildlife (970) 725-3557
Copper Mountain Over the Hill Gang
Copper Mountain Nature Center
    (800) 458-8386 ext 2
Ducks Unlimited, Summit County Chapter
    (303) 369-3925
Friends of the Eagles Nest Wilderness
    (970) 453-9056

Frisco Historical Society (970) 668-3428
Keystone Science School (970) 468-5824
Rocky Mountain Elk Foundation, Central
    Rocky Mt. Chapter, (800) Call- Elk
Sierra Club, Blue River Group, Rocky
    Mountain Chapter, (970) 468-2002
Summit County Open Space Advisory
    Council, (970) 453-2561
Summit County Open Space & Trails
    Department, (970) 547-0681
Summit Historical Society (970) 453-9022
Summit Huts Association (970) 453-8583
Summit Recycling Project (970) 668-5703
Trout Unlimited, Gore Range Anglers Chapter
    (970) 668-0176
U. S. Forest Service, Dillon Ranger District
    (970) 468-5400
Vail Pass Task Force (970) 468-5400
White River National Forest Association,
    Summit (Arapaho Forest) Chapter,
    (970) 468-5400

PHOTOGRAPHER'S DATA

Most of the photographs in *Spirit of Summit County* were taken with a Nikon N90 camera body and a variety of Nikon lenses. Beck's most used lenses are AF Nikkor 80-200mm, 1:2.8 D; AF Micro Nikkor 105mm, 1:2.8; and AF Nikkor 28mm, 1:2.8. She uses a Gitzo tripod when necessary due to low light or desired depth of field, and extension tubes are occasionally used for close-ups. Filters and fill-flash are not used. Beck's films of choice are Fujichrome Velvia and, more recently, Provia.

She usually shoots at aperture priority.

Although she takes advantage of the auto focus technology, she focuses manually for her flower photography, for other selected nature shots, and usually when on a tripod.

The thin air and brightly reflective sun and snow of the high altitude require bracketing and experimenting. Try to see the light!

A number of the photographs in *Spirit of Summit County* are available as Fine Art prints. Contact PrismLight Press for information.

INDEX OF PHOTOGRAPHS

Numbers refer to photo number, not page number.